Magical Animals

Retold by

CAROL WATSON

Illustrated by

NICK PRICE

CONTENTS

Series Editor: Heather Amery

Reading Expert: Betty Root
Centre for the Teaching of Reading
University of Reading

The Terrible Griffon

The Griffon lived high up in the rocky hills, but when it was hungry it flew down to the valley to look for food.

A farmer called Ahmed lived in the valley. He had lots of animals but his favourites were two fine oxen.

Once upon a time in a far-off land there lived a gigantic monster. It had a head and wings like an eagle and a body like a lion. It was called a Griffon.

The Griffon was a very powerful creature. It had the strength of a hundred eagles, and just one of its enormous claws was as big as a lion's head.

The oxen were big and strong with large horns and shiny coats. Ahmed was very proud of them and he used them to plough his fields.

One day, when Ahmed was out ploughing, he saw a large black cloud in the sky. As it came nearer he saw that it was not a cloud but the Griffon flying down. "Help!" he cried and he ran out of the field. The Griffon grabbed the oxen in its great claws and flew off with them.

3

"My poor oxen," Ahmed wept. "That horrible monster will eat them." "We will go and kill the beast," said his friends.

A few days later Ahmed and nine brave men set off to find the Griffon. They were armed with bows and arrows.

The men climbed high up into the rocky hills. Suddenly Ahmed saw a skeleton. "Look," he said sadly, "it must be one of my oxen." "Come on," said his friends. "Perhaps the other one is still alive and we can save it."

They went on until they came to a strange tree. "That's not a tree," said Ahmed. "It's an enormous feather. The Griffon must be nearby."

4

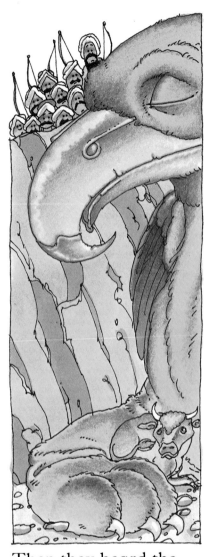

Then they heard the sound of very loud snoring. The men peered over the cliff and saw the Griffon fast asleep. The ox was still there.

"Now's our chance," whispered Ahmed. The men fired their arrows into the Griffon, and with a terrible roar it fell back dead. They rescued Ahmed's ox and took it home. When they heard the Griffon was dead everyone in the valley cheered. They were so happy they bought Ahmed a new ox, even better than the first one.

5

Pegasus the Winged Horse

Long ago in Greece there lived a handsome young prince called Bellerophon. He was strong and brave.

The King of Greece hated Bellerophon and wanted to kill him. He thought of a plan, then he sent for the prince.

"You must prove to me how brave you are," he said. "You must kill the Chimera, the terrible monster which keeps eating my people."

Everyone in Greece was frightened of the monster, so Bellerophon went off to find it. On his way he met a strange old lady.

The lady was a fortune teller. "Beware of the Chimera, Bellerophon," she said. "Before you fight the monster you

must catch Pegasus, the winged horse. It can fly like a bird and if you ride on its back you will be safe."

The old lady told the prince where to find Pegasus and he went up into the mountains. At last he saw a beautiful white horse. It had huge wings and was galloping wild and free. "How can I catch it?" thought Bellerophon.

Suddenly there was a flash of light in front of him and the goddess Athene appeared. She had come to help the prince.

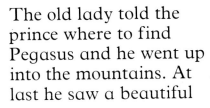
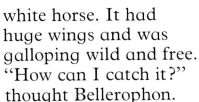

"Take this bridle," she said. "It is magic. Put it over the horse's head and Pegasus will become quiet and tame."

The prince bowed low. "Thank you, goddess," he said and took the bridle. Then he waited behind a rock near a river. When Pegasus came down to drink, he crept up behind the horse. Then he gently slipped the bridle over its head.

7

At first the horse struggled and reared, but very soon it was calm and let the prince leap on to its back.

"Now I will fight the Chimera," cried Bellerophon. The horse spread its huge wings and rose up into the sky.

They flew to the place where the Chimera lived. The air was hot and steamy and there was a horrible smell everywhere. Suddenly, out of a cave came the monster.

8

The Chimera was half goat and half lion. It had two heads, and the lion's head breathed fire like a dragon.

Instead of a tail there was an enormous snake. It spat at Bellerophon, trying to kill him with its poison.

"Fly down, Pegasus," cried the prince and he fired his arrows at the monster. The lion roared and huge flames shot out of its mouth. The heat was awful and the smoke made them cough.

"Fly up quickly," called Bellerophon. They flew above the flames so the monster could not hurt them. The prince fired more and more arrows until at last the Chimera grew weak.

9

Bellerophon went back to the king. "I have killed the man-eating monster," he said. "Your kingdom is safe."

"This will kill it," thought the prince. He took out his spear and stuck a lump of lead on the end. Then they flew down once more and the lion opened its mouth to roar. Bellerophon thrust his spear down the lion's throat. The flames melted the lead inside the monster and it screamed and wailed in pain. Then it fell down dead. The boiling lead had killed it.

The people cheered Bellerophon and said he was a hero. Some even said he must be a god and worshipped him.

10

Zeus, the king of the gods, was very angry when he saw Bellerophon riding towards Mount Olympus. He sent a bee which stung Pegasus. The horse reared up and Bellerophon fell off. He fell down to the earth below and was killed.

Soon the prince began to boast and think he was a god. He decided to fly to Mount Olympus, the home of the gods. He rode off on Pegasus.

"That is what happens to people who think they are gods," Zeus laughed. He caught the flying horse and took it to Mount Olympus. For ever after that Pegasus lived with the gods and pulled the chariot of Zeus across the sky.

The Evil Cockatrice

Long ago there lived a poor farmer called Zak and his wife, Beela. They were so poor they had no animals at all.

All they had were a few old hens and a skinny cockerel, and all they had to eat were the eggs that the hens laid.

One day the cockerel started crowing loudly and walking round and round in circles. "That's odd," thought Zak.

The cockerel sat on the ground and ruffled his feathers. "He's acting like a hen," said Beela, looking puzzled.

Then an extraordinary thing happened. The cockerel laid an enormous egg, and ran off flapping its wings.

A few minutes later there was a tapping sound and the egg cracked. A tiny head pushed its way out.

When the cockerel saw what it was it screamed and fell on the ground. It rolled over in the dust and died.

Zak and Beela were horrified. Out of the egg came a small snake which sat up proudly and looked around.

It had yellow and black skin, bright red eyes and a cock's comb on its head. "It's a cockatrice!" screamed Beela.

13

A cockatrice was an evil creature which only came to life when a cockerel laid an egg. This was very rare.

Its breath was deadly and it burned everything it touched. As it moved, the grass withered and the rocks cracked.

A large rat ran out of the grass. It stopped suddenly and looked at the cockatrice in surprise.

The cockatrice turned to look at the rat with its horrible red eyes. The rat screamed and fell down dead.

Anything that looked at the cockatrice died. "We must warn everyone," cried Beela and they ran off to the village.

They went to the chief of the village and asked him what they should do. "We must kill the beast at once," he said.

A brave soldier offered to kill the cockatrice. "Do not look into its eyes or you will die," Beela warned him.

"I will wear a helmet to protect my eyes," said the soldier. He blindfolded his horse and took his lance.

Soon he came to a field which was burnt and black. "The cockatrice must be near here," thought the soldier.

Then he saw it. The cockatrice slithered along the ground towards him, with its red eyes glowing.

The soldier galloped up to it and stabbed it as hard as he could. "Die, you evil beast," he shouted bravely.

As the point of his lance touched the snake, the soldier felt a terrible pain in his hand and he dropped the lance.

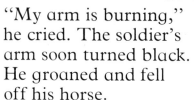

"My arm is burning," he cried. The soldier's arm soon turned black. He groaned and fell off his horse.

He lay on the ground and did not move. The soldier was dead but the evil cockatrice was still alive.

The horse slowly found its way back to the village. "What has happened to the soldier?" cried Beela.

When they found the soldier was dead, Zak and Beela were very frightened. They went to the priest. "How can we kill a cockatrice?" they asked. The priest looked in an old book. "It will die if it sees its own reflection," he said.

16

"We need a large mirror," said Beela. They bought one in the village, then they went off to find the beast.

They carried the mirror to the place where the cockatrice lived. Then they hid behind some rocks and waited.

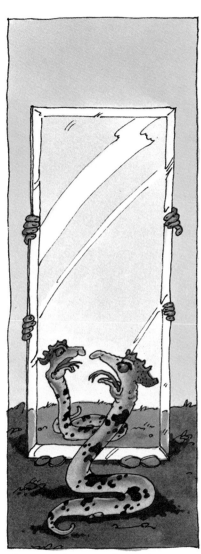

Soon the cockatrice appeared. Holding the mirror in front of them, they walked towards it. It stared at itself with its horrible red eyes.

Suddenly there was a piercing scream. Zak and Beela peeped round the mirror, and there on the ground the evil cockatrice lay dead.

The Beautiful Unicorn

If a king or queen owned a magic horn they knew who was good and who was bad, and who their secret enemies were.

The King of Scotland wanted a magic horn. "Find me a Unicorn," he said to his servant, Toby. "And bring it back to me."

Once upon a time there was a very rare and precious creature called a Unicorn. It had the body of a sleek white horse, the legs of an antelope and the tail of a lion. But most important of all was the horn which grew on its head. It was a magic horn and people all over the world tried to find a Unicorn so they could use its horn to have power over others.

18

"Where am I going to find a Unicorn?" Toby thought. He set off on his horse and travelled across many lands.

Toby searched for years and years but he could not find a Unicorn. He was old and tired but he dared not return home.

"There is only one place I have not tried," he thought. He went up into the lonely mountains of Tibet.

He stopped at a village and met an old man. "Have you ever seen a Unicorn around here?" Toby asked.

"The Unicorn only appears when it sees a beautiful young girl," said the man. "Shama, my grand-daughter, has seen one. She will lead you to it." The next day Toby met Shama and they set off. "It's a long journey," she said.

Shama led Toby further up the mountains to a lonely place. The air was still and the moon seemed to shine more brightly in the sky.

"If I take you to the Unicorn you must not kill it or harm it in any way," said Shama. "It is a very special creature."

At last they stopped near a wood. Shama called out and whistled softly. Then quietly, out of the trees, came a beautiful Unicorn.

The magic of the Unicorn cast a spell on Toby and he did not want to catch it and take it to his king.

So Toby went home without a Unicorn. "I have failed you, Sire," he said, and told the king what had happened.

It trotted over to the girl and knelt in front of her. She sat down and it put its head on her lap. Toby could not believe his eyes.

"If I can't have a real Unicorn," said the king, "I shall have them on my Coat of Arms." From then on there were two unicorns on the king's royal banner. He took them with him wherever he went, though they had no magic powers at all.

21

The Enormous Kraken

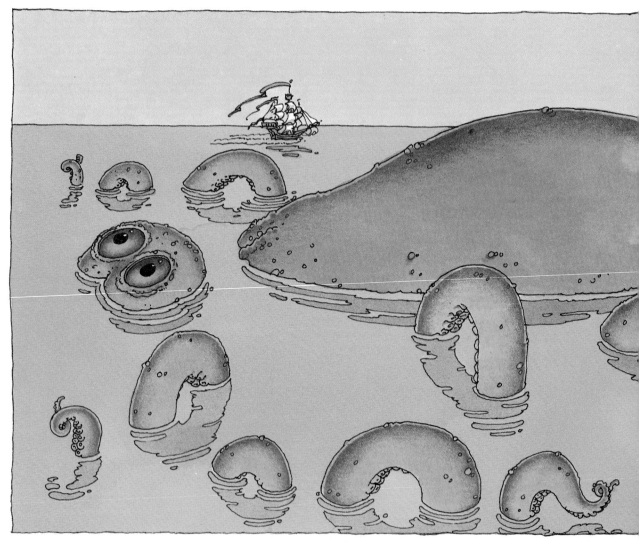

Many years ago there was a huge sea creature called a Kraken. It was nearly two miles wide and had hundreds of long tentacles.

Although it was so big the Kraken was quiet and gentle. It never tried to harm anyone unless they got in its way or hurt it.

The Kraken usually lived at the bottom of the sea. If it ever did come to the top, it clung to some rocks and stayed there for a long time.

Sometimes it stayed in one place for so long that sand blew over it and trees and shrubs grew on it. It looked just like land.

One day a sailing ship dropped anchor near a small island. "I've not seen this island before," said the Captain.

"Let's explore it," he said. So the sailors rowed to the island in small boats. They took lots to eat and drink.

When they reached the shore they were very hungry, so they lit fires and roasted some meat. They drank their wine and told stories. The more they drank, the noisier they became and they danced and sang all night long.

23

Suddenly the ground trembled and shook and huge waves crashed on to the beach. "It's an earthquake!" screamed the sailors.

But it was not an earthquake, it was the Kraken waking up. The sailors had landed on the monster, and their fires had hurt it.

The Kraken waved its tentacles and plunged to the bottom of the sea. All the sailors were drowned and the monster was never seen again.